CHILDREN AND PARENTS BEATING NIGHTTIME FEARS

A Parents Guide

DR. JONATHAN KUSHNIR
RAM KUSHNIR

Children and Parents Beating Nighttime Fears

By: Dr. Jonathan Kushnir, Ram Kushnir

Annie is nine years old. Ever since she was little, she hasn't been able to fall asleep unless at least one of her parents stays by her bed. She never learned how to fall asleep by herself. In recent months, she has started talking about fears at night. She tells her parents that she is afraid of thieves, frightening clowns, and being alone. Every night when she goes to bed, one of her parents sits next to her, and she constantly talks to them. If they go out of the room, she calls them over and over. They go back to her room, sit for a while, and talk to her. Then they leave the room and tell her to go back to sleep. As a response, she demands they stay in the living room with the TV on. Many times, her father gets upset and shouts at her to "go to bed already." Her mother is startled by the shouting and sits next to Annie until she falls asleep.

This is a common going-to-bed description of a family with children who experience nighttime fears, a phenomenon that manifests itself in distress before going to bed and during the night. This difficulty disrupts the sleep of children and parents and can harm the family's daily life.

Annie and her parents are not alone. Many children see the night and "going to bed" as an anxious experience, in a way that makes them feel distressed. Most of the time, the child's family suffers from her anxiety as well.

The complementary children's book *Benny Goes to Bed on His Own* is designed to help parents do the following:

- convey relevant information on nighttime fears and coping strategies to children in a story-friendly way
- create a dialogue with the child about "the issues surrounding their sleep difficulties"

- establish with him or her an orderly and effective plan for dealing with fears, based on cognitive-behavioral-therapy

For the past fifteen years, I have treated thousands of children and adults with anxiety and sleep difficulties, while conducting clinical research in these fields. This experience enabled me to accumulate the knowledge and develop strategies to successfully help parents and children cope with nighttime fears and sleep difficulties. I hope that this knowledge will help you and your child overcome their fears and bring more peaceful nights.

In this book for parents, we have added a broad background on fears and anxieties and, specifically, the phenomenon of nighttime fears.

We have also expanded the explanation of the tools on which this intervention is built, used in cognitive-behavioral therapy, and the way to communicate this to the child, along with examples and exercises.

Please note that this book is not a substitute for treatment by a qualified professional.

1—Introduction

FEARS AND ANXIETIES IN CHILDREN—BACKGROUND

Many children suffer from significant fears and even actual anxiety disorders but are often undiagnosed and untreated. The problem is that these difficulties can greatly disrupt the quality of life and functioning of the child and his or her family. It's therefore very important to pay attention as early as possible in case a significant difficulty exists, and consider consulting with your child's pediatrician or a health-care provider to address his or her difficulties.

Significant Fears and Anxiety Disorders in Children

Significant anxiety disorders and fears are among the most common disorders in children and adolescents (Kessler et al., 2005), and they can have a negative effect on a variety of areas in the child's life and family life. Without treatment, these severe difficulties may persist for a long time and even worsen. In many cases, children will suffer from several fears, or even several anxiety disorders or other difficulties at the same time. Despite the high prevalence and significant negative consequences, anxiety disorders in children and adolescents are often undiagnosed and untreated. Early detection and accessibility of effective treatments can significantly reduce the negative impact of the child's difficulties and lead to an improvement in his or her self-esteem.

Nighttime Fears

For many children, the process of going to sleep and falling asleep can be challenging and become stressful, especially for young children. This happens for a number of reasons:

- significant separation from parents
- disengagement from family life
- being alone
- dealing with darkness and its negative link to "evil forces" (e.g., criminals, ghosts, evil)
- the experience of loss of control

All of these can be related to nighttime fears.

Moderate and time-limited nighttime fears are a very common phenomenon, and are part of normal development, with most children and parents overcoming it without much difficulty. For many children, however, great and lasting difficulty arises.

The content of fears changes as age increases and as the child develops. Infants and very young children fear things that are here and now (e.g., separation from parents), kindergarten-age children show fears of more imaginary things (e.g., monsters), and older children have more realistic fears (e.g., burglars) (King et al., 1997).

Nighttime Fears and the Sleep of Children and Parents

The sleep of children with significant nighttime fears may be disrupted. They have difficulty falling asleep. They wake up many times at night and have difficulty falling asleep again after waking up. Disrupted sleep can harm functioning in kindergarten or school, increase anxiety or behavioral difficulties, and impair cognitive function.

Even the parents' (ineffective) coping in trying to reduce fears can impair the children's sleep quality. In addition, parents' sleep can also be disrupted as a result of their coping methods or their attempts to solve the problem, or both. This sleeping disruption can affect the mood of the parents, the relationship with the child, the parents' own relationship, and their daily functioning at home and at work (Kushnir and Sadeh, 2011).

Ways of Coping with Nighttime Fears

Research shows that children say they use all sorts of ways to deal with their nighttime fears, such as seeking parental support and clinging to animal soft toys or other objects as well as a variety of other behaviors (Gordon et al., 2007).

However, usually, the most important aspect in fighting nighttime fears is the way parents react. The presence of the parents at the child's bedside at bedtime or in response to fears during the night is a very common way of coping as an attempt in reducing the child's fears. Some parents also allow their children to sleep in their bed. This coping strategy can also lead to positive results in many cases. However, it may perpetuate, preserve, and increase both the fears and the adoption of this method of coping. In fact, many parents have not planned to rely on this way as a long-term solution, but some find themselves using it over time because of the continuation of fears or their escalation.

When children go to bed very worried, they need one of their parents to lie next to them until they fall asleep. The family members become "hostages" of the child's fears and difficulties. They are "forced" to behave in a certain way so that the children will calm down and eventually fall asleep. Parents also worry that if they don't behave in that way, the whole night will become a nightmare, and they won't get to sleep either.

Bottom line, these coping methods actually sabotage children's abilities to develop calming ability on their own, so that children rely on their parents as a way of calming down—leading to increased fears and continued difficulty.

In *Benny Goes to Bed by Himself: Kids and Parents Beating Nighttime Fears Together*, we describe that this is exactly what happened to Benny and his parents. Benny feared imaginary creatures every night. Over time, the method in which his parents sat next to him until he fell asleep became established. They were exhausted and frustrated, the fears continued, and Benny learned that he was incapable of falling asleep on his own

Signs of a Significant Problem

The following signs indicate that your child may have a significant problem with nighttime fears.

- The child shows extreme reactions before going to bed or when waking up at night—crying, physical signs, sadness, anger, frustration, hopelessness, embarrassment.
- The child asks repeated questions for confirmation that express concern at night, such as "What will happen if a thief comes?" He or she won't accept logical arguments, and it will be greatly difficult to comfort him or her.
- The child will regularly have headaches or abdominal pain before bed.
- The child exhibits anxiety that arises before going to bed.
- The child shows signs of a sleep disorder—difficulty falling asleep, dependence on parents, multiple awakenings, recurring nightmares.
- The child avoids sleeping outside his or her home, like at friends, on trips, or with relatives.
- Parents spend a lot of time comforting the child due to fears at night, in bed, or during waking hours.
- The problem lasts for several weeks or months.

In the next sections, we will describe several coping methods to address these difficulties.

2—Fears—Components and Characteristics

THE FEAR RESPONSE

The fear response will appear in a situation where we think we're in danger or in a threatening situation. These reactions will occur not only in a situation of real "danger" but also in a situation where there is a perception or thought that the situation is dangerous. Beyond the frightening thoughts that arise, as part of the body's normal response to this condition and preparation for dealing with it, there are all sorts of sensations that appear, for example, accelerated pulse, sweating, rapid breathing, and more. The last component of the fear response is the behavioral component. What do I do in response to a "threat?" Do I run away (flight) or fight?

Let's look at an example where a child (also relevant, of course, for an adult) is afraid of dogs. In that case, when the child sees a (normal) dog on the street, he or she will have a scary thought. The child will be convinced that the dog is going to bite him or her (even though the dog is actually busy sniffing trees and has no awareness of the child). The fearful child will have a physical reaction that will prepare his body for coping with the danger. He or she will choose to walk away or hide behind parents (avoidance) or use a "safety object," such as a stick (fight). These feelings and thoughts disappear as soon as the threat is "eliminated" and the child isn't bitten.

This is a very important point. From the child's perspective, the child perceives that he or she was "saved" (because the child was not bitten), but actually, the fear was strengthened, and his or her belief in his ability to cope was reduced. The child didn't learn that the result would have been the same if he or she hadn't walked away.

Returning to Benny, when Benny went to bed every night, he had frightening thoughts about all kinds of creatures, and unpleasant sensations in his body followed. He tried to solve this problem by thinking "happy" thoughts (thinking is also "behavior"), and his parents "had to" sleep next to him to help him be less afraid and fall asleep.

Why Fears Persist

Let us return to the example of the fear of dogs. As soon as the child thinks that the danger no longer exists (i.e., he or she leaves what he or she perceives as the dangerous location, or hides behind his or her parents, or obtains a safety object—the stick—to defend himself), the unpleasant feelings diminish, the perception of danger slowly disappears, and he or she feels safe. He or she believes, because of his or her avoidance or the fact that the child had a safety object, that the dog didn't bite him or her. Although in the short term, he or she will think and feel that he or she is "saved," the problem is that he or she won't learn that dogs are not dangerous (usually) and that the child isn't able to cope differently with this kind of situation. Therefore, every time he sees a dog, these symptoms return. In addition, after a period of time of relaxation, most children (and adults) realize that their reactions were excessive. Moreover, seeing other children pass by the dog without any problem might even hurt their moods and their self-esteem.

Safety Behaviors and Safety Objects

We can regard the evasive and defensive behaviors and use of security objects as the collection of tricks and methods that children (and adults) use in response to the frightening thoughts and feelings that arise.

The purpose of these safety behaviors and objects is (at least, that is the belief) to reduce the "danger" that the child believes he or she is in, and also, to lower the feeling of anxiety. This relief is very rewarding. The problem is that it is one of the main factors that contribute to the preservation of frightening/threatening thoughts, feelings, and a sense of inability to cope with the situation. Although in the short term the child (and his or her parents) feel relief, over time, they enter a vicious circle that only contributes to the continuity and even strengthening of anxieties. The problem is that the child and his or her parents continue to behave in the same way over and over again without reaching a direction of healing and a path that will liberate them from this vicious circle. This resembles someone's car stuck in dirt while the driver presses the gas harder and harder to get out. The result is that the car is dug deeper and deeper in the dirt.

In Benny's case, he tries to think "happy" thoughts. This leads to a rebound effect that only causes the frightening thoughts to return after a short time, even though sometimes it leads to a temporary and brief decrease in anxiety. In addition, he and his parents performed a repetitive ritual every night during which they had to stay by his side until his fear was reduced and he fell asleep. Benny didn't learn how to cope alone, and he didn't learn that what he feared didn't really occur when one of his parents was not present. He also didn't learn that the physical warning signs (e.g., shallow breaths and a pounding heart) don't herald danger. In addition, Benny's parents didn't learn that Benny was able to cope despite the difficulty.

In conclusion, this way of coping, although it helped Benny fall asleep every night, was established over time and didn't help Benny and his parents find a direction that would help him and them overcome the problem.

A List of Common Safety Behaviors in Nighttime Fears

The following behaviors are common among children with significant nighttime fears:

1.The parent's presence as a means of calming down.

2.Sleep with your face to the wall so as not to see the door and closet, or sleep facing the door to see that no one is coming.

3.Sleep only with a sibling in the room.

4.Sleep with the blanket over the head ("I am protected").

5.Clogging "holes" by the bed with pillows ("Nothing can come out of it").

6.Sleep only with lights on.

7.Listen to music (to prevent hearing noises).

8.Do not close your eyes (to prevent scary thoughts).

9.Only going to bed before the parents.

10.The parents must be in a specific place and not go to sleep until the child falls asleep.

3—Parental Role

THE ROLE of Parents

Parents play very critical and significant roles in the development of their children's emotional and behavioral world. They can design an environment in which the child's difficulties will be manifested, aggravated, or even created. But they can also shape the environment so that the child will need to confront and overcome his or her fears and difficulties.

As children grow older, the challenges they face get more complicated. This makes the parents' ability to influence increasingly difficult. If we continue to adapt to the child's problems instead of teaching the child to cope on his or her own, we contribute to the perpetuation of the child's difficulties. If we direct our behavior in a completely different way in the face of his or her fears, we can actually direct the child on a path of growth. This will help the development of extremely important coping abilities for life.

Many parents of children who suffer fear-and-anxiety disorders feel great frustration, anger, and despair in trying to cope with their children's difficulties. Many times, each parent takes a different position in coping attempts. This leads to a lot of friction and tension between the parents. The main point is that many times parents continue to behave exactly the same way for a long time in an attempt to help their children (and themselves) to solve the problem. They double down on a method that has not helped so far. The result is that the child suffers, the parents suffer, and the situation doesn't move in the direction of resolution or improvement.

Parenting Styles

Generally speaking, there are two parenting styles when talking about parents of children with fears.

1. The protective parent. Driven by the thought that the child is suffering badly and needs to be cared for, they pad the child so that he or she suffers as little as possible. These parents "solve" the difficulty for the children, reinforce the avoidance of situations that frighten the child, and don't encourage the child to deal with the difficulty. That is, the parents shape the child's environment in a way that will serve the fear and not allow the child to cope. The problem with this style is that it doesn't allow the child to grow, to deal with the fear, to learn that coping is actually an option, to learn that it can be overcome and that the "danger" doesn't materialize in most cases. Even if there is an unpleasant result, it remains unpleasant and isn't a catastrophe.

2. The demanding parent—a parent who has unreasonable demands from the child in dealing with his or her fears. This parent doesn't "see" the child and the child's distress, doesn't give legitimacy to the child's difficulties, sometimes also humiliates the child ("What is your problem?" "It's just…" "You're acting like a little girl…," "Anyone can overcome it."). This style is driven by the illusion that the

child can just "get out of it." The parent assumes that what the child thinks is nonsense and even an attempt of manipulation by the child. The main problem with this style is that now the child is dealing with two problems not just one; i.e., the fear itself and also the confrontation or disappointment from his or her parent that comes with it. This style has a substantial contribution to the child's nonurgency to cope, and a deeper entrenchment, in which the child will hide and won't agree to face his or her fears and cope.

Often, the parent will have his or her dominant style, but the mix of styles and parent reactions can vary according to the situation; for example, a mother who adopts a protective style but at night, because of disrupted sleep, adopts a demanding and aggressive style in the face of the child's fears. Another problem arises when each such parent doesn't agree with the style the other parent adopts. The child is stuck in the middle, and this can potentially mount further difficulties to the already dire situation.

The goal is to get the parents to work together, as one parent-style body in which the child's distress is seen and treated and not disregarded, but in no way "cooperated with." The parents' job is to work together in order to give the child a boost and a direction of dealing with the difficulty. The message is of coping, of growth, and of parental respect and support.

Parental Conduct

Most often, out of a desire for the child to fall asleep quickly, or as a result of pity for the state the child is in, parents stay close to the child or the parent stays in the child's bed. This serves as a way to deal with the child's fear and can lead to a quick falling asleep. As mentioned, in the short term (overnight or for a few hours), it can help. However, in the long run, this behavior may preserve the condition. This doesn't allow the child to learn that he or she is capable of dealing with fears, creates dependence on the parent, and doesn't allow the child to learn that even if the parent isn't around him, the frightening thing won't happen. In addition, the child learns that the frightening feelings "require" that a parent stays next to him. Finally, the going-to-sleep time for children who have a strong parental dependency will be prolonged, and the number of nocturnal awakenings will increase. The child won't learn that he or she is able to fall asleep alone.

On the other hand, many parents show anger out of frustration and demand illogical things from the child. This leads to a worsening of the condition, a feeling of humiliation, and the child will have a harder time coping with his or her fears and being able to fall asleep. It can also bring a lot of stress to the parent-child communication.

In general, the right response is to give validation to the child's fears: "I know it's hard for you, sweetie," and aim to execute an orderly and gradual plan of properly dealing with the child's fear.

Benny wanted very much to fall asleep alone, fight his fears, and not be dependent on his parents. He had a hard time with bothering them at night. But still, this conduct went on and on.

Important Questions

1. Do I continue to behave exactly the same way in the face of my children's difficulties?
2. Has it helped so far, or is the situation actually getting worse?
3. How long have I been telling myself that eventually the difficulties will pass?
4. What value/parental message do we give to a child in this way?
5. What happens if no change is made?

When trying to resolve the problem, the first and foremost goal is to help the child and his or her parents understand that the coping methods they've tried so far don't lead to the solution of the problem and even worsen it. Next, the goal is to explore and incorporate other, adaptive and effective, ways of coping. This will be shown in later sections.

4—Key Cognitive-Behavioral Tools

IN THIS SECTION, we'll describe the main effective methods that can be used by children and parents to deal with nighttime fears and accompanying sleep difficulties.

How to Begin Talking to Our Children about "Fears"

A great way to start discussing fears in general and fears at night in particular with our child is while reading the book *Benny Goes to Bed on His Own: Kids and Parents Beating Nighttime Fears Together*. The book describes in a simple and child-friendly way what "fear" is, what excessive fear is, why fears remain, and how to deal with them effectively. If you don't have the book, you can start a discussion with your child about whether fear is good or bad.

Explain that fear is very important and helps us in a wide variety of situations in life, like looking right and left before crossing a road, wearing a seat belt, and a host of other examples. But sometimes fear appears in situations where it should not appear, and then we think, feel, and act as if there is a real danger, even though none really exists.

The previous sections in this book, "The Fear Response" and "Why Fears Persist," can be used to explain the fear response and the components of fear to demonstrate why exaggerated fears remain and also, the way to deal with them.

The following sections describe the therapeutic tools used in the program of dealing with night fears.

Externalization

One of the tools that can help a child is *externalization*, that is, creating a difference between reality and the frightening thoughts a child has. Giving a name to the frightening process will help the child treat fear as something external to him that can and should be dealt with. In Benny's story, he chose the name Tricksy, but you can give all sorts of names to the scary thoughts that come up before bed, for example, the bully, the monster, grumpy, stupid, and so on.

It's possible to develop a conversation with the child, not while going to bed, when you are alone with him or her, and say something like, "We've noticed that you have scary thoughts that worry you and keep going around in your head and don't leave before bedtime (appendix 1 can be useful for and your child make a list of his/her fears). We know these are really scary thoughts, and we know they feel real, but it's very important to remember that these are real thoughts that are in your head but are not necessarily true in reality. It's as if you have someone chattering in your head. Let's give this person a name."

With smaller children (if suitable, with older ones as well), you can ask them to draw this character (see appendix 2).

Self-Talk

One of the tools that can help children deal with their fears during the gradual program is self-talk. The main aim isn't to calm the child down with this self-talk but to help a child begin to behave in a way that will help him deal with the fear and not perpetuate it. For example: "I won't let fear defeat me," "It was scary at first, but if I face it, it will slowly disappear." When it got a little hard, Benny used to say to himself, "If I stay strong and don't give up, Tricksy's nonsense will stop."

Parents should sit with the child, not while going to bed, but at an earlier time, and go through a variety of "sayings" with their child. Parents can use the phrases as described or use any idea that they think of or their child thinks can be useful above (see appendix 3). They should encourage the child to use these "sayings" at night when they feel that fears arise.

It's also possible to simulate the use of this tool during the day. The child can practice or simulate using the sentences while lying in his bed. After reciting these sayings with the child, it is intended that the child will use this tool at bedtime and, if necessary, also during the night.

Challenging Scary Thoughts

Another tool that can be used is trying to challenge the thoughts. The aim is to help the child ask questions that will assist him or her in dealing with the frightening thoughts and carry out the behavioral plan. Once the child realizes that "Tricksy" (or any other name he or she chooses) appears in the child's head at night, he or she can use the technique of challenging and/or asking questions that help deal with him.

For example (in this example, fear of witches):

1. How many times have I been afraid that a witch would come in at night, and how many times did one actually come in?
2. Will a witch really come, or is that just a thought Tricksy put in my head?
3. What happened the last time I was afraid the witch would come?
4. Am I able to deal with my fear of the witch?

5. If my parents are not close to me, will a witch really come?
6. If my parents are next to me, does it prevent the witch from coming, or does it strengthen Tricksy?

Parents can sit with the child and help the child think about these or any other questions that can help him or her deal or challenge the frightening thoughts.

You can also try to encourage the child to use this technique by pretending to be detectives, scientists, researchers, or mystery-solvers. After going over the questions with the child, parents can encourage the child to use this tool at bedtime and, if necessary, also during the night. It's also possible to simulate the use of this tool during the day when the child is awake but lying in bed, pretending it's night time and practicing (see appendix 4).

Dealing with Scary Thoughts and Parental Dependence

Process-wise, this is the heart of the intervention in helping the child to cope with the difficulties.

Like any learning in life, coping with fears should be done gradually, increasing the intensity step by step. For example, if I want to start jogging, I can't start with a ten-mile run. I will start with routine walking and then try running while gradually increasing the length (and maybe the speed) of the run. The challenges presented to the child as part of this process should be such that he and his parents can withstand despite the particular feeling of fear.

When dealing with nighttime fears, almost in all cases, the goal is to reduce the child's dependency on the parents, which serves as his or her calming factor, and to teach the child to cope with the fright-ening feelings and thoughts by him- or herself. This self-coping will lead the child to fall asleep independently.

A good path to start a discussion about the plan is after reading the book about Benny, and making a plan that will be "as Benny and his parents did." Present a story to the child about learning to ride a bike (or any other relevant example that their child will be personally familiar with that would require stages/steps). Point out that this begins with removing the training wheels and the parent holding the bike while the child is riding. Then gradually, the parent stops holding the bike for longer periods of time while the child succeeds in riding longer and longer without the training wheels or the parent holding the bike. During this process, the child's fear of riding the bike declines, and confidence grows.

As described in Benny's story, at first, the parents move slightly away from the child's bed until he falls asleep, and every two or three nights, after a certain level of security has been achieved, they gradually move away from the child's bed.

Parents should explain to the child (not at bedtime) that they will begin fighting the child's fear gradually, one step at a time (appendix 5 can be helpful in order to make a gradual plan). For example, "We are going to start fighting your fears at night together, but we'll do it in a very gradual, manner. First, we're going to gradually start sitting farther and farther away from you, but we won't leave till you fall asleep. After several nights, we're going to sit a bit farther, but again, till you fall asleep. We're going to continue this way till you will be able to fall asleep when we sit by the door."

The instruction to the parents is to not respond to the child's "requests" from the moment they decide to "turn off the lights and go to sleep."

After making progress, when it is clear that it's getting easier for the child to fall asleep and the parent has reached the door, the parent can begin to go out and enter the room at set times, with intervals that lengthen every two to three nights, until the child falls asleep.

At the end of such a period of time (defined by the parents and the child), the parents "check" the child for a very minimal period of time, a few seconds. They can give the child a kiss, fix the blanket, show themselves, but immediately leave the room and not interact. The parents continue these short visits until the child falls asleep. Between visits, the parents don't communicate with the child, even if the child tries to. It's important to avoid getting into a discussion or conversation around the child's fears. Although, in fact, the presence has a certain calming effect, the intention is to direct the child to cope so that he or she can overcome the fears without the presence of a parent. The message is that we're here, giving a small anchor (visiting) but directing you to cope by yourself.

The conversation with the child at this stage can be something like, "We are very proud of you. We continue to fight your fears together, but from tonight, we're going to go to sleep a bit differently. When we say good night, we'll leave the room and come back to check after X minutes. We'll do that again and again till you fall asleep. Every several nights, we'll increase the time between the checkups. We'll do it till you can go to sleep by yourself and get rid of Tricksy forever. If it gets a bit scary, use the questions and statements we practiced."

The time between checks will depend on the age of the child, his or her temperament, and the difficulty of the parent in implementing this plan.

In order to strengthen the child's engagement, you can also draw stairs or a ladder with the child, and on each step, indicate the task to be achieved (for example, the parent enters every five minutes).

It's very important to carry out the plan consistently, night after night, even if there are some setbacks with an increase in difficulty along the way. If the child gets out of bed between the checkups, parents should try returning him or her calmly to the child's bed. However, if this behavior continues and the child continues to get out of bed, parents should reduce the time between checkups, so it will be easier for the child, and after a period, when they see the anxiety reduces, they can prolong the time between checkups.

It's important to note that every child and family has their own "rhythm," depending on the child's fear level, parental coping style and ability to implement the plan. Thus, there are cases where progress will be made quickly (even days), and others may take weeks or even months.

Thanks to the gradual process, Benny developed a capacity for self-calming. Thus, he was able to overcome his fears and, as a result, fall asleep independently. He also began to sleep alone, without waking up regularly every night.

What Happens with Nocturnal Awakenings

It's important to emphasize that the most significant predictor of nocturnal awakenings is parental dependency on going to sleep. Children who are dependent on their parents will wake up more and will need the same conditions at night (parent presence) to deal with the fear and fall asleep during the night.

Many times, we suggest that parents begin to implement this plan only during the going-to-bed period, without changing anything during the night wakings. Many times, in parallel to the improvement during bedtime, parents should expect an improvement during the night, such as reduction of fears, reduction of night wakings, and in the child's ability to fall asleep on his or her own after the child wakes up.

If there's very little or an unsatisfactory improvement during the night wakings, the same gradual plan can be applied also when the child wakes up during the night.

What Is Achieved in Therapy

In this type of work, which is done in a gradual but very focused manner, while the parents gradually push the child, a sense of ability develops in the child. The child no longer feels that he or she is a victim of the fear. The child and parents learn about the gap between their black (catastrophic) thoughts and what is actually happening. The child sees that the feeling of fear doesn't stay forever, and it passes when coping and not while using avoidance.

Parents learn a lot about the parental role and can apply it to a variety of other situations. The parents learn that their response has a very significant weight, such that it can push and strengthen the child's ability to cope.

Parents learn that by changing their own behavior and the way they relate to the child (such as punishing, speaking aggressively, humiliating and demanding, or supporting avoidances), they can greatly and positively influence their child's behavior and the way the child copes with his or her fears. The child learns that the environment doesn't conform to his or her demands and doesn't adapt itself to the child, but he or she has to deal with the difficulty him- or herself.

This is exactly what happened to Benny and his parents as a result of the gradual and determined process they performed in their gradual distancing from him. Slowly, Benny developed the confidence that he could cope without his parents, including the confidence that he could succeed on his own. Benny was less managed by his thoughts, and the feelings of anxiety diminished until he finally succeeded in falling asleep on his own and was happy.

Along the process, you can monitor your child's gradual progress and fear level in every stage using appendix 6.

The scale's range is 1–5, where 1 is the least scared and 5 is the most scared.

Important Points to Emphasize

- It's very important that both parents make a joint decision that they are going to carry out the process in full and go forward even if obstacles arise. It's advised not to begin if one of the parents isn't sure or has reservations about dealing with the problem. A joint decision will allow parents to optimally execute the program and succeed.

- During the process, there may be increases and decreases in the child's feeling of fear. This is normal. It's very important to continue and be consistent. Let the fear adapt to the new framework and not let us, the parents, continue to adapt to the fear.

- If you see that a certain level is too difficult for you or for the child, don't get alarmed. Simply lower the level of difficulty and raise it again after you see improvement.

- Consistency at work is extremely important for success. If we don't persist, we'll immediately return to the old habits. At best, we'll postpone progress, but at worst, we won't be able to progress at all. The message must be very clear and consistent.

- Both parents should be full partners and provide the same environment for the child. When the parental message is clear (and accurate), the chances of progressing will greatly increase. When the parental message is unclear, or even contradictory, there's no joint work, and this will greatly hurt the process.

- The parents should talk to each other and share their concerns about the program. Examine how one parent can help the other during the process. For example, if implementing the program is difficult for one parent (because of the parent's concerns) he or she can ask the other parent to do it first or even to replace the other parent on a certain night. Another example is that if one parent is unable to refrain from expressing anger and frustration toward the child while going to bed, he or she will ask the other parent to replace him or her in the process.

- It's important to remember the parent is like a captain at sea, steering the ship in a storm. If he or she stands calmly, handing out simple and clear instructions, inspiring confidence, it will help the sailors do the job well and get through the storm. When the parent is stressed, angry, accusing, it will be very difficult to get through this storm.

Why Distractions Do Not Work and Exposure to Scary Thoughts

Some of the methods children (and adults) use to try to control the frightening thoughts in order to relax (or that's what their parents told them to do) are attempting distractions, trying to think "good" thoughts, and trying to stop worrying.

In fact, these ways may lead to very temporary relief from anxiety, but in the long run, the result is potentially a significant increase in the anxious and frightening thoughts.

Why is this happening? Here's a little experiment:

1. For the next three minutes, do your best not to think of a pink rabbit standing on a rock. Notice what happens during the exercise. What is the result? Did you manage not to think about the rabbit, or did he jump into consciousness several times?
2. Now, in the next three minutes, try to do the opposite. Do everything you can to think of this rabbit. Do it as strongly as possible. Please see if during the exercise the picture starts to fade, if something in it changes, or if other thoughts pop up. What was the result?
3. Now, in the next three minutes, watch your thoughts. If thoughts of a pink rabbit pop up, stay in the role of a viewer/observer. Do not do anything with the thought. Be passive. See this thought as part of a general landscape of

thoughts. Just another one of the thoughts/images you have in your mind. What is the result?

When we try to make an effort and not think about something, there is a rebound effect where we think about it a lot more. On the other hand, if you try to think of something proactively or take an observer role, it is difficult to maintain it. Similarly, children who constantly try not to think about the worrying thoughts, both by behavioral attempts at thought (like distraction) and by seeking closeness to the parent, will actually experience a perpetuation and amplification of these frightening and worrying thoughts.

In carrying out the gradual plan of the parent moving away and the child self-coping, we're actually helping the child to stay with his or her frightening thoughts and, thus, over time, help the child deal with them. We actually lead the child to have a different "relationship" with frightening thoughts, thus, to stop giving the thoughts "negative power," and so over time, there is a decrease in their frequency and intensity and, as a result, a decrease in anxiety.

Exposure to Scary Thoughts

Another way that scary thoughts can be dealt with is by a deliberate exposure and dwelling in the frightening thoughts.

Take, for example, a child who is very afraid of ghosts when he or she is lying in bed. Every night when the child goes to bed, he or she tries to take breaths, be distracted, talk to his parents, or any other way that would help the child not think of ghosts. He or she knows that ghosts don't exist, but still, come nighttime, it scares the child very much.

Our goal is that the child will deal well and effectively with the thought itself. The way to do this is gradual and planned exposure to thoughts. This should not start at bedtime.

How do we do that?

1. We'll start by building a scare scale going from 1 to 10, where 10 is the scariest, and 1 is the least scary.
2. The child will need to rate the scare level for a set of scare items, to which he or she will be exposed. An example for fear of ghosts:

- Item 1: Thinking about the word *ghost*, example rating: 5.
- Item 2: Seeing a drawing of a ghost, example rating: 6.
- Item 3: Saying the phrase, "Maybe a ghost will come at night," example rating: 8.
- Item 4: Saying the phrase, "A ghost will surely come at night," example rating: 10.

For very young children, you can build a simpler scale of "easy," "medium," "hard."

1. We'll build the scale with the child and implement the exercise with the child at a comfortable hour, not in the evening, and surely not before going to bed. The chosen time should be one that the child and his parents regard as relatively not scary (i.e., he or she is less likely to have an anxious reaction to the items mentioned earlier). Usually, morning or noon are well-suited times.
2. Repeated exposure—starting.

We'll sit with the child at the chosen time and go over the least scary item. If the least scary item is pronouncing the word *ghost*, we'll ask the child to repeat that word over a period of a few minutes. After one minute of the child pronouncing the word, we'll ask him or her to indicate the scare rate. It's expected that, at first, the scare level the child experiences will increase, and at some point, it will start decreasing and continue downward. We'll stop this exercise either once we see a substantial decrease in the scare level the child indicates or after twenty minutes.

We'll repeat this as a daily exercise with the least scary item until it is clear that this exercise is easy for the child and there is minimal or no anxiety.

1. Repeated exposure—moving up the scare ladder.

Once we exhausted the first level (fear level is around 1–2), we can move up the ladder, and expose the child to the scarier items. We can repeat this exercise and continue moving up the ladder.

Gradually, it will be easier for the child to be with the thought at night because he or she is learning that he or she is able to deal with these scary thoughts with the help of practice.

1. Repeated exposure—moving to a later time.

Since the impact of the frightening thoughts increases the closer they are to bedtime, we can further move up the scare ladder by exposing the child to the scary items at later hours. For example, after the child has successfully accomplished this exercise at noon with item three (maybe a ghost will come at night), we can request him to do that at 5:00 p.m. Eventually, at an advanced stage, we can implement this exercise when the child goes to bed.

This method can be used in parallel to the behavioral plan at night.

Courage Boxes

Another way to give a boost to the process and direct the child to coping is to prepare a courage box together. The child can use this box to indicate and preserve his or her achievements in moments where the child successfully dealt with their fears. This can be used for various areas of achievements, not only overcoming nighttime fears.

We write a note with the date and description of what the child did and put it in the box.

At a family meal on the weekend, you can open the box and show off to everyone how the child coped and what he or she did. You can also call the grandparents, or any other role model that the child will be happy to share his or her success, and read the notes aloud to them.

5—An Example of Coping Procedure

DAN AND JENNY are parents to seven-year-old Tiffany. For several months now, Tiffany has been having a very hard time falling asleep at night. She absolutely must have one of her parents close to her when she goes to bed. She really needs physical contact; otherwise, she won't be able to relax and fall asleep. Tiffany says she's afraid that witches and ghosts will come. Even though in the morning she says she doesn't believe they exist, at night, it feels to her as if everything is very real. At night, she would wake up and call one of her parents, who would come and lie next to her.

Dan and Jenny have already "tried everything," giving her prizes, using a monster catcher, using an "anti-monster spray," and drawing a painting of the monster and tearing it. They tried to talk to her about it many times, explained at night that there are no monsters, hugged her tight, and sometimes even got upset and angry at her. Tiffany felt very bad about everything that was happening and really wanted to solve the problem.

So far, nothing had worked, and there had been much frustration.

They decided to try the proposed approach in the book *Benny Goes to Bed by Himself*.

In the afternoon, they sat together and read the book to Tiffany. She listened enthusiastically. They asked her if she wanted to cope with the problem like Benny did. She agreed, and they decided to build a similar plan.

That night, they sat next to her, but they didn't make any physical contact. She tried to talk to her parents to calm her down, but they occasionally repeated the phrase "Good night, sweetie. Go to sleep. We won't let Tricksy win this time."

It was a little hard for Tiffany, but after a while, she fell asleep. After a few nights, when it got easier, they gradually started to move away from her bedside. They kept increasing the distance from her bed every few nights until they were sitting at her room's door. There were sometimes easier and sometimes more difficult nights, but her parents strictly stuck to the plan and didn't let her fear run them. Each morning, Tiffany would get up happy, and Dan and Jenny would mark in a special chart how far from her bed they sat last night.

When Tiffany had a difficult night, she used self-talk: "I can handle it!" or she used questions such as "How many times did I fear the monster would come, and how many times did it actually appear?" "Will the monster come tonight, or is that one of Tricksy's blabbers in my head?" After several nights of Tiffany falling asleep when her parents sat at the door, they began to do repeated short checks. They would show up at the door every few minutes, smile silently, and leave. Every few nights, they increased the interval between these checks, and they would continue these checks until she fell asleep.

Her parents, although sometimes losing patience, did everything exactly according to plan, didn't get upset and urge her to go to bed, and didn't enter into endless conversations to reassure her like they used to.

In parallel, Tiffany's parents started working with her gradually on exposure to scary thoughts on a daily basis.

They also made a courage box together and gathered more and more notes.

In time, Tiffany's parents saw that it took her less time to fall asleep. During that period, she came to their bed less and less during the night and called them to her own bed fewer times. Still, there were nights where her fears got the best of her, and she'd wake them up. At one point, when they saw that the middle of the night awakenings were continuing, they began implementing the going-to-bed plan for night wakeups as well. When she called them, they would simply apply the short check exercise, visit her every few minutes but not sleep or sit next to her. They would continue these checks until she fell asleep. Over time, they increased the interval period between checks during the night as well.

Sometimes, they would call her grandparents and read the notes from the box.

Eventually, after several weeks, there was no more need for bedtime checks, and Tiffany even told them that one night she woke up and didn't need their help to go back to sleep, and so it went on.

Tiffany's sleep got better, she got up more refreshed, and her parents were also fitter during the day. They were very proud of her for her coping (please see appendix 7 for a flowchart of the process).

6—Frequently Asked Questions (FAQ)

Q: Do the fears go away?

A: Usually, children will have fears at one stage or another, and this is a normal developmental process. These fears will go away after a short period of time and without significant impact. In some children, however, the fears won't go away. They'll even worsen; lead to great distress; and impact the child's functioning, his family, and the relationship between them.

Q: Is it possible to leave a small light on?

A: Generally, it is possible to leave a small light on, but direct it toward the floor so that it doesn't interfere with the child's sleep.

Q: Is it possible for the child to sleep with the parents sometimes?

A: Allowing the child to sleep with the parents "sometimes," similar to sleeping with the parents every night, perpetuates the problem. During the intervention, a gradual plan is conducted to help the child cope with his or her fears and gradually be able to sleep in his or her bed alone.

Q: Will buying a better bed or mattress solve the problem?

A: The problem in this case isn't related to the quality of the bed and mattress. It won't solve the child's night fears.

Q: Can this process harm the child?

A: There is no evidence that such a process causes harm to a child. There is ample evidence that such a successful process can also lead to a reduction in fears, a reduction in sleep difficulties, improved parent-child communication, and more.

Q: Why not just sit by the child and calm him down?

A: As mentioned, calming the child can sometimes be a short-term solution (for a specific night), but in the long run, using this method will lead to dependence on the parent and perpetuation of the problem.

Q: Should both parents be involved?

A: It's highly recommended that both parents be involved in the process for a variety of reasons. First, both parents can learn about the importance of changing their behavior in helping the child. Second, there are many situations where at a given moment, only one parent is at home. It's very worthwhile for both parents to be able to manage the process. Third, the message is very clear to the child when both parents behave the same way. Fourth, it's some-times difficult for one parent for all sorts of reasons to perform the process at a certain time (apprehension, fatigue, frustration), and in order to have a continuum, it is important that both parents can be involved.

Q: Will it help to be stricter with the child?

A: As explained in the previous sections, a "demanding" parenting style leads us to "erase" the child's difficulty and put him in a stressful position with his parent in addition to his original fears, so the difficulty increases and the path to coping becomes much more difficult.

Q: Do fears return after they go away?

A: Fears love to try and come back even after a very successful process. They mainly recur in stressful situations, crises, life changes (changing a school, moving homes), quarreling between parents, and for a variety of other stressful reasons. It's very important in such a situation to recognize that the difficulties are back and to immediately return to the principles learned here in order to prevent the process of deterioration and return to the previous situation.

Q: What about sleeping over?

A: For many children who suffer from nighttime fears, this is a significant difficulty. You should turn to dealing with this difficulty after successfully coping at home. Once the child feels comfortable sleeping at his own home, sleepovers become much easier.

Q: Is it worth giving OTC drugs?

A: The psychological difficulty with these drugs is that they often become safety objects. That can lead to the child becoming "addicted" to the "problem-solving" drug and doesn't lead to coping in a different and effective way. This is why such drugs are not only unhelpful but become a major factor in maintaining fear.

Q: Is it possible that the child is just being manipulative?

A: Many parents are afraid that the child is "manipulating," but when there are clear signs of anxiety (crying, distress, dependence on the parent), it certainly indicates a difficulty that requires gradual intervention to deal with the fear and certainly not criticizing or implying that it is manipulation.

Q: Can certain things in a child's diet make fears worse or have a negative impact on sleep quality (e.g., sugar, caffeine, etc.)?

A: It's advised not to consume products that contain caffeine (such as tea, coffee, chocolate, etc.) several hours before bedtime, as these products can lead to difficulties falling asleep. Eating a big meal close to bedtime is also not advisable for the same reason. However, to the best of our knowledge, there is no correlation between diet and fear level.

Q: Should my child avoid watching TV, tablets, smartphones, and so on before bedtime?

A: It's advised that children stop watching all kinds of screens at least an hour to an hour and a half before bedtime, as this can significantly impact the child's ability to fall asleep at the desired time.

Appendix 1

CHILD-PARENT JOINT ACTIVITY: Describe Your Fears

This is where the child can share his or her scary thoughts.

. . .

"When I go to sleep, I am afraid of:"

_____

_____

_____

_____

_____

_____

_____

_____

Appendix 2

CHILD-PARENT JOINT ACTIVITY: Externalization

This is where the child can draw and give a name to his or her storytelling "bully."

(In Benny's case, it was Tricksy.)

My storytelling bully's name is:

_____

_____

_____

And this is what he looks like:

Appendix 3

CHILD-PARENT JOINT ACTIVITY: Self-talk

This is where the child can get inspiration and write his/her own self-talk phrases.

Some self-talk examples:

1. *I won't let fear defeat me!*
2. *It was scary at first, but if I face it, it will slowly disappear.*
3. *If I stay strong and don't give up, Tricksy's nonsense will soon stop.*

And here you can write your own self-talk phrases:

_____

_____

_____

_____

_____

_____

_____

Appendix 4

CHILD-PARENT JOINT ACTIVITY: Challenging the Scary Thoughts

This is where the child can ask questions that challenge the scary thoughts.

He or she can use these provided questions and add new questions of their own.

1. *How many times have I been afraid that _____ would come in at night, and how many times did one actually come in?*
2. *Will a _____ really come, or is that just a thought Tricksy put in my head?*
3. *What happened the last time I was afraid _____ would come?*
4. *Am I able to deal with my fear of _____?*
5. *If my parents are not close to me, will _____ really come?*
6. *If my parents are next to me, does it prevent_____ from coming, or does it strengthen Tricksy?*

And here you can write your own questions:

_____

_____

_____

_____

_____

_____

_____

_____

Appendix 5

CHILD-PARENT JOINT ACTIVITY: Gradual Progress Log

This is where you and the child can log each night's plan before going to bed.

For example:

"Night 1: Mom will sit by the dresser/door"

...

"Night 12: Dad will check on you every five minutes."

_____

_____

_____

_____

_____

_____

_____

_____

_____

_____

_____

_____

_____

_____

_____

_____

Appendix 6

CHILD-PARENT JOINT ACTIVITY: Monitor the Fear Level

Use this scale of 1–5, where 1 is the least scared, and 5 is the most scared.

We can use this scale to track the child's gradual progress. The goal is to reach as low a level as possible.

How scared am I? (Point out the level that fits most)

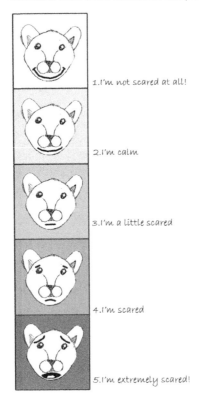

1. I'm not scared at all!

2. I'm calm

3. I'm a little scared

4. I'm scared

5. I'm extremely scared!

Appendix 7

Flowchart of the process

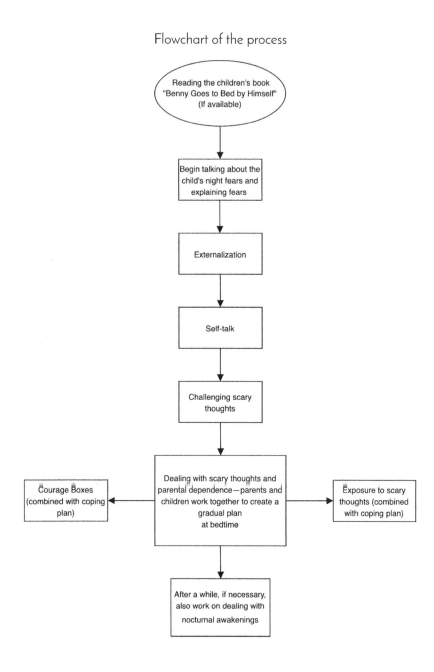

References

1. Kessler R. C., Berglund P., Demler O., et al. (2005). "Lifetime prevalence and age-of-onset distributions of DSM-IV disorders in the National Comorbidity Survey. *Archives of General Psychiatry* 2005; 62:593–602.
2. King, N., Ollendick, T. H., & Tonge, B. J. (1997). "Children's nighttime fears." *Clinical Psychology Review, 17*(4), 431–443.
3. Kushnir, J., Sadeh A. (2011). "Sleep of preschool children with night-time fears." Sleep Medicine, 12, 870–874.
4. Gordon, J., King, N., Gullone, E., Muris, P., & Ollendick, T. H. (2007). "Nighttime fears of children and adolescents: Frequency, content, severity, harm expectations, disclosure, and coping behaviours." Behaviour Research and Therapy, 45(10), 2464–2472.

Made in the USA
Las Vegas, NV
23 January 2024